Flannery O'Connor's Georgia

Flannery O'Connor's Georgia

Photographs and Text by Barbara McKenzie

Foreword by Robert Coles

The University of Georgia Press   *Athens*

Copyright © 1980 by the University of Georgia Press
Athens, Georgia 30602

Designed by Richard Hendel
Set in 12 on 14 point Mergenthaler Janson type
Printed in the United States of America

Library of Congress Cataloging in Publication Data

McKenzie, Barbara.
    Flannery O'Connor's Georgia.
    Includes bibliographical references.
    1. O'Connor, Flannery—Homes and haunts—Georgia—Pictorial works.
2. Georgia—Description and travel—1951–   —Views. I. Title.
PS3565.C57Z76   813'.54   80-10936
ISBN 0-8203-0517-0
ISBN 0-8203-0518-9 pbk.

Foreword

There has been no shortage of critical response to Flannery O'Connor's all too brief but truly inspired writing life. She has prompted over a dozen critical books, and many dozens of essays or reviews. Some of her readers are taken with her theological sophistication: they want to show how shrewdly she has worked it into her stories and novels. Others, more literary-minded, have found her one of the most compelling masters of fiction this country has produced in recent decades. And then, there are those who connect her resolutely, and often enough with a touch or more of condescension, to the South: yet another strange writer with a strange name from that strange region. Of course, she felt inclined to give the definitive back of her hand to that last breed in a wonderful essay "Some Aspects of the Grotesque in Southern Fiction"; and the words no doubt reflect a few moments of indignation on her part: "I have found that anything that comes out of the South is going to be called grotesque by the Northern reader, unless it is grotesque, in which case it is going to be called realistic."

Maybe this book will be called grotesque by some who leaf quickly through its pages—pictures that stress God; fowl; a not especially populated landscape; oddly ornamental old homes; and people preoccupied with dousing their fellow human creatures in water, or worrying about nothing less than the very end of this planet. As a Yankee college freshman I taught wrote in a paper a few years ago: "I don't understand those people in those stories." Later, in a conversation, he asked me this boldly: "Why do they have those funny names—Carson, Eudora, Harper, and Flannery?" Eager to be psychological—no original direction, alas, these days, he had this connection in his mind: "Maybe their funny names make them want to imagine things."

I have seen even cruder and more fatuous "psycho-historical" explanations, though I must say I didn't dare probe the reasons such a link was made, for fear, maybe, of meeting up with—well, the grotesque. It is so easy for any number of us to reserve for our lives, our physical and mental and moral landscape, the designation of "normal" or "appropriate," leaving for others various thinly disguised reprimands, expressions of patronization or scorn. Flannery O'Connor, in fact, came from a distinguished and cultivated family. She lived in a state whose cultural traditions go back to the first days of this nation's history. She drew her personal strength from a broad range of the West's intellectual life. She lived in a country whose gently rolling hills, rich farmland, and complex, interesting village life are, in sum, a match for what can be found anywhere in the United States. And her neighbors, in Milledgeville proper or out Andalusia way, or anywhere else in Georgia, struggle with the same problems that confront those who live in New York's Manhattan or California's Marin

County, not to mention Cambridge, Massachusetts: how ought one live this particular life we happen to have, and what does it mean, actually—if anything?

To be sure, there are regions in this large and diverse country. And this book shows an aspect of one of those regions—rural and small town South, Georgia division. But Flannery O'Connor was no ordinary person—in the sense that her mind was given the largest possible spiritual and creative leeway, it seems, by that "fate" we all puzzle over and try to figure out. She did belong, though, to the people she lived near—belonged to them in the sense that they entered her everyday life, in one way or another; and also, entered her fiction—dominated it, in fact. In story after story, in both novels, she called upon Georgia's yeomen, its small town folk, its rural preachers and God-haunted believers, its citizens and workers and souls. They are not enough, of course, to account for the O'Connor fictional canon; she was a (pure if not so simple) genius. But no writer, however inspired by his or her visions and voices, lives apart from a given world. The task of a critic is to reflect upon, report upon the elements of a particular achievement. This book's author-photographer, Barbara McKenzie, fulfills that responsibility wonderfully—with tact, intelligence, and originality. We'll never know what enabled a certain Milledgeville woman to give us those pieces of unforgettable fiction; but some of the nourishment, it can be said, that she called upon is presented in these pages—a modest but quite instructive contribution to many of us for whom Flannery O'Connor's presence in this century was a moment, all too brief, of grace.

Robert Coles

Acknowledgments

A book of photographs, more than most books, is truly a collective effort, and I would like to acknowledge the following persons for their contributions to this book. Mrs. Regina Cline O'Connor for her generosity in allowing me to copy photographs from the Flannery O'Connor Memorial Room and to photograph at Andalusia and the Cline House; Gerald Becham, curator of Special Collections at the Georgia College Library in Milledgeville, for his research assistance, unfailing kindness, and belief in this project. John Taylor, Gail Nicholson, Rob Williams, Clate Sanders, and Annette Haywood for accompanying me on my photographic journeys through Georgia and listening to my ideas. My parents, Leslie and Euphemia McKenzie, who understood the importance of this book from the beginning. Stanley Lindberg and Betty Sargent of the *Georgia Review* for their steadfast support of my photographic endeavors. Ken Cherry, formerly of the University of Georgia Press, who helped shape this project initially, and Iris Tillman Hill, whose astute editorial judgment gave this book its final form. And ultimately, the people of Georgia who let me reflect their individual lives and their collective wisdom.

Introduction

I

This book of photographs began almost twenty years ago when I first drove to Milledgeville, Georgia, to interview Flannery O'Connor. On that trip from Tallahassee, Florida, through south and middle Georgia, I watched the landscape change. The Spanish moss gave way to bare trees (for it was late winter); signs nailed to trees advertised their province as Christ or a restaurant 500 yards up the road; pitted, gullied red-clay banks thrust up to the macadam highway; brick chimneys stood as silent markers of vanished houses. I scanned the countryside, as I drove, trying to penetrate beyond the highway images. I was looking at this land, I realized, not through my eyes alone but through a vision superimposed by Flannery O'Connor's fiction. She was my silent companion in the car.

On that February afternoon in 1962, Flannery O'Connor and I talked about her understanding of "country." In an essay she had written that "country" is "everything from the actual countryside that the novelist describes, on to and through the peculiar characteristics of his region and his nation, and on, through, and under all of these to his true country, which the writer with Christian convictions will consider to be what is eternal and absolute."[1] Flannery O'Connor wrote of the "true" country inside the writer's country, and this is her most remarkable achievement.

When her illness, the rare form of lupus that caused her death in 1964, had occasioned her return to Milledgeville in 1951, she and her mother, Mrs. Regina Cline O'Connor, chose to live at Andalusia, a 500-acre farm. At the time of my visit, Andalusia was "in the country," well beyond the city limits. Today the city extends beyond the borders of the farm itself, and a Holiday Inn sits across the highway, welcoming newlyweds, civic groups, and conventioneers alike.

That winter of 1962, while working on a dissertation on contemporary American women authors, I wrote to Flannery O'Connor, requesting an interview, to which she graciously consented. She met me in the "back parlor" of the farmhouse, a comfortable, light, and airy room containing a large walnut bookcase with glass doors, a sofa placed against a far wall, tables holding books and magazines and small ornaments, a wicker chair, and a rocker. With equal graciousness she answered my questions. I was then concerned mainly with uses of region in her fiction. I knew she didn't like being called a regional writer: "The woods are full of regional writers," she had written, "and it is the great horror of every serious Southern writer that he will become one of them."[2]

1. Flannery O'Connor, *Mystery and Manners: Occasional Prose*, edited by Sally Fitzgerald and Robert Fitzgerald (New York: Farrar, Straus and Giroux, 1970), p. 27.
2. *Mystery and Manners*, p. 29.

After I asked the last of my questions, our conversation drifted toward more general topics, punctuated by O'Connor's dry wit and satirical eye. I soon discovered that laughter was a kindred spirit for us. Later that afternoon I was invited to tour the farm. The farms in Flannery O'Connor's fiction are almost always versions of Andalusia with its white two-storied house standing on the crest of a hill and its ponds and pastures and enveloping woods. I was impressed by the many kinds of animals there, the cows, donkeys, chickens, roosters, geese, swans, and the forty peafowl. The peacocks upstaged all the other animals, not because their plumage or domineering, strutting presence insisted upon our notice but because they seemed so out of place on this Georgia farm. That night at dinner both O'Connors told stories about life in Milledgeville, and I realized that incidents and characters in some of the fiction came from conversations similar to those I was hearing, reminiscences between mother and daughter, or anecdotes recalled by Mrs. O'Connor, who is herself a superb storyteller.

Soon after my arrival in Athens, Georgia, in 1967 I began to use my camera to record the tangible dimension or physical reality of Flannery O'Connor's fiction. My search for backwoods prophets and fundamentalists similar to those portrayed in her fiction led me to water baptisms and numerous tent revivals and camp meetings. At first, I was unsure of my welcome, but I was received with uniform cordiality on all these occasions. I photographed the frenzied motions of persons seized by the Holy Ghost, and my camera was not felt as an intrusion, I soon realized, but as a tribute; perhaps it was even more than a tribute: it was providing tangible proof of the mysterious workings of the Holy Spirit.

Because my conversations with Flannery O'Connor had reinforced my awareness of her as a comic writer, I set about deliberately to use photography to show the grotesque as one source of her humor.

"I think I shall write," Calhoun tells his great aunts in "The Partridge Festival."

"Well," his Aunt Bessie said, "that's fine. Maybe you'll be another Margaret Mitchell."

"I hope you'll do us justice," his Aunt Mattie shouted. "Few do."

By Aunt Mattie's standards, these photographs fall short of doing justice to middle Georgia. This area is prettier than the photographs reveal, its people more solidly middle class; its highways more orderly; its cities more progressive. But my intention is not to promote tourism in Georgia any more than it was O'Connor's goal.

For Flannery O'Connor the grotesque was a way of getting beneath the surface prettiness of things to reach "closer to the heart of the matter."[3] My photographs are

3. Sr. Mary-Alice, O.P., "My Mentor, Flannery O'Connor," *Saturday Review*, May 29, 1965, p. 24.

an attempt to translate Flannery O'Connor's grotesque fiction into visual images. Through single images or the juxtaposition of multiple images I try to suggest pictorially the comic and violent look of her fiction.

II

Flannery O'Connor's Georgia is really two Georgias. She belonged to the upper class in a small town that is fiercely proud of its old houses and old families. Milledgeville was the capital of Georgia from 1807 to 1868, and history hangs heavy in the air and on the walls; it breathes its inanimate life under glass, it decorates rooms, it has organizations to bolster it, it is there for the reading on roadside markers or for the observing on guided tours of the old Governor's Mansion. Sherman and his troops passed through Milledgeville on their march to the sea but elected not to destroy the city.

Dominating Milledgeville with its central rotunda rising fifty feet to a domed ceiling is the impressive Governor's Mansion. Equally impressive but more approachable is the Cline House, adjacent to it, where Flannery O'Connor lived as a girl and where her mother lives now, a house that also had the distinction of serving as the temporary Governor's Mansion in the 1830s while construction was going on next door. Situated close to the tree-lined street, the Cline House does not impose itself upon visitors, and its porches, fluted white columns, and spacious high-ceilinged rooms give it a wonderful authenticity; the house stands as a visual tie to the past.

"When you get well," the mother tells her ailing son in "The Enduring Chill," "I think it would be nice if you wrote a book about down here. We need another good book like *Gone with the Wind*." The son could feel the muscles in his stomach begin to tighten. "Put the war in it," she advised. "That always makes a long book."

Flannery O'Connor put the war in only one story, "A Late Encounter with the Enemy," and in it history (at least the emptiness of some of our rituals that attempt to preserve and glorify the past) becomes a source of humor. She also chose to give only brief glimpses of the cultured, genteel small-town society she knew intimately. The reason may be simple: the rural poor served her purposes best. So did persons maimed in body and spirit. So did the backwoods preachers and prophets. I think the distinction between the Georgia she knew by birth and upbringing and the Georgia she chose to write about is very important. Readers often confuse the two, and in so doing they fail to realize that Flannery O'Connor was exercising a literary prerogative: "The writer can choose what he writes about but he cannot choose what he is able to make live, and so far as he is concerned, a living deformed character is acceptable and a dead whole one is not."[4]

But the confusion between the reality of Flannery O'Connor's life and the imagined life depicted in her fiction continues to exist, supported by the knowledge that, like many of the educated sons and daughters of the farm owners, she was physically impaired, dependent upon her mother, and "over-educated." The photographs taken in her maturity contribute to this confusion. In newspaper and book-jacket photographs, we see her scowling intently at the camera, or leaning on crutches, engaged in some bucolic pastime like feeding the peacocks or geese that adorned the lawns of Andalusia. The photographs are often unflattering and depict her as stern and ill-tempered. The truth of the matter is that Flannery O'Connor did not like being photographed and, as it turns out, had little use for photographers. "I hate like sin to have my picture taken and most of them don't look much like me, or maybe they look like I'll look after I've been dead a couple of days," she wrote to a friend. A short while later she complained that "any jerk can take a picture of you and do with it what he wills. I am sure there are now in existence hundreds of horrible pictures of me that I have no control over. Your face ought to be sacred to you but it sure is not. . . . Photographers are the lowest breed of men."[5]

Flannery O'Connor was a private person and being photographed constituted an invasion of privacy that she found distasteful. Furthermore, she was not deluded about the physical changes that illness and the medication she was taking had caused. In describing her self-portrait, she explained, "I was taking cortisone which gives you what they call a moon-face and my hair had fallen out to a large extent from the high fever, so I looked pretty much like the portrait. When I painted it I didn't look either at myself in the mirror or at the bird. I knew what we both looked like."[6]

Mary Flannery O'Connor was born March 25, 1925 in Savannah, Georgia, to Edward Francis and Regina Cline O'Connor. Childhood photographs show a beautiful child who, in the words of a family friend, was also "beautifully cared for." The family photographs reprinted here are from a collection at the Flannery O'Connor Memorial Room at the Georgia College Library in Milledgeville. After I had seen them I knew that I had to add them to my own book of photographs of Flannery O'Connor's Georgia. I felt that they would give balance to the world I was presenting, for I had begun to see my own pursuit of the people and countryside of the fictional world as an injustice to the author. In my own way I was contributing to the distortion of other readers and critics who did not keep in mind

4. *Mystery and Manners*, p. 27.
5. *The Habit of Being: Letters of Flannery O'Connor*, edited by Sally Fitzgerald (New York: Farrar,

Straus and Giroux, 1979), pp. 524–25, 534.
6. *The Habit of Being*, p. 525.

O'Connor's two worlds. In my photographs I concentrate on the vivid landscapes and characters of her fiction; but here we can see Flannery O'Connor growing up in a different Georgia.

The first of the photographs is from a series of studio portraits taken when Flannery was about two years old. The family chose one from this series for their Christmas card that year. In 1937, when it was discovered that Mr. O'Connor was seriously ill with disseminated lupus, the O'Connors moved to Milledgeville, where the Cline family had lived for more than a century. The cortisone drugs that retard the progress of lupus were not available at that time, and Mr. O'Connor died of the disease in 1941, while Flannery was a student at Peabody High School in Milledgeville. In 1942 she enrolled at Georgia College for Women, also in Milledgeville, where among other activities she worked on *The Corinthian*, a quarterly literary magazine. Graduating in 1945 with a Bachelor of Arts in Social Science, she attended the Writers' Workshop of the University of Iowa, then under the direction of Paul Engle, receiving her Master of Fine Arts degree in 1947. In 1949, after living at Yaddo in Saratoga Springs, New York, and in New York City, she moved to Connecticut to live with Sally and Robert Fitzgerald and their children. Her stay with the Fitzgeralds was cut short by illness when, late in 1950, it was discovered that she was suffering from disseminated lupus. Her first attack was so severe that her life was in danger. But the new cortisone drugs, mainly ACTH, aided her recovery, and after several weeks in hospitals she was able to convalesce at home.

Flannery O'Connor left Connecticut with the first draft of *Wise Blood* almost

Flannery, age two, and her mother, Regina
Cline O'Connor. Flannery was a happy and
beautiful child who, in the words of a family
friend, was also "beautifully cared for."

Flannery, age three. The intense concentration and furrowed brow were also to be characteristic of her as an adult.

completed and with a contract for its publication from Harcourt, Brace and Company. While she was hospitalized and later at home, she revised the manuscript, following changes offered by Robert Giroux, her editor at Harcourt, and suggestions by Caroline Gordon, a writer the younger author admired. The publication in 1952 of *Wise Blood* did not go unnoticed in Milledgeville, although it seems the book itself went largely unread by the general populace.

Neither Regina nor Flannery O'Connor had experienced farm life on a daily basis until 1951 when they moved to Andalusia, which was then a working dairy farm. But mother and daughter prospered in their new setting, with Mrs. O'Connor running the farm with great verve and dedication, and Flannery O'Connor continuing to write, a daily activity interrupted only by periods of illness or visits to colleges and universities where she lectured on the craft of writing. In 1955

Flannery, age seven, on the occasion of her First Communion. Flannery favored her father in appearance and her resemblance in this portrait to Edward O'Connor is striking.

A Good Man Is Hard to Find, a collection of short stories, was published. Five years later she published *The Violent Bear It Away*, her second novel. The farm provided the solitude she needed to write and to rest, for always she had to conserve her energies for the important task of writing. She continued to write until her death on August 3, 1964.

III

Flannery O'Connor chose to write about the uneducated and rural poor rather than about persons of her own class and education; but I do not mean to suggest that she was unfamiliar with the life she depicted in her fiction. On the contrary. Milledgeville is a small town (in 1978 the total population was 12,000), and like

Flannery, age twelve. Mrs. O'Connor, an excellent seamstress, made Flannery's clothes. Here Flannery looks much as she did in her early twenties.

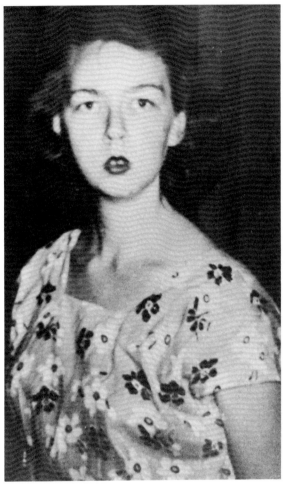

Flannery, age sixteen or seventeen. As a teenager, she continued to write stories and to draw, becoming particularly adept at caricature and cartoon.

most small towns it harbors few secrets and many eccentrics. Life in the Cline House did not keep Flannery O'Connor from firsthand acquaintance with the nearby farms and their occupants. Living at Andalusia only made that acquaintance more intimate. Letters to friends are full of references to the goings-on at Andalusia. "I don't know how long they [a farm family] will be with us but I am en-joying it while it lasts, and I aim to give my gret reading audiance a shot of some of the details sometime. Every time Regina brings in some new information, our educ. is broadened considerably." Her remarks about Milledgeville are much more subdued. An invitation reads, "We expect you to visit again in Milledgeville, a Bird Sanctuary, where all is culture, graciousness, refinement and bidnis-like common

Flannery, college years. Flannery attended Georgia College for Women in Milledgeville, graduating in 1945 with a Bachelor of Arts in Social Science.

Flannery worked on The Corinthian, *the quarterly literary magazine of the college. She's pictured here on the porch of Parks Hall with the editor of the yearbook, 1944.*

sense." Life on the farm was anything but subdued. In fact, in a letter to Elizabeth Bishop, she wrote, "I am glad to say that most of the violences carried to their logical conclusions in the stories manage to be warded off in fact here—though most of them exist in potentiality."[7]

Sometimes the concept of a story came from an outside source. She credits an advertisement in Milledgeville's weekly newspaper, the *Union-Recorder*, for an incident that led to one of the chapters in *Wise Blood* (1952). A local theater was offering free passes to moviegoers willing to shake hands with a gorilla appearing "in person" the day of the film's showing.[8]

7. *The Habit of Being*, pp. 41, 209, 198.

8. From an article in the *Milledgeville Union-Recorder*, April 25, 1952.

Flannery, college years. From 1945 to 1947 she attended the Writers' Workshop at the University of Iowa, receiving her Master of Fine Arts in 1947.

Flannery, 1952. This photograph, taken after her first bout with disseminated lupus, was used on the book jacket of the first edition of Wise Blood.

The genesis for "The Artificial Nigger" (1955) came from direct observation:

Well, I never had heard the phrase before, but my mother was out trying to buy a cow, and she rode up the country a-piece. She had the address of a man who was supposed to have a cow for sale, but she couldn't find it, so she stopped in a small town and asked the country-man on the side of the road where this house was, and he said, 'Well, you go into this town and you can't miss it 'cause it's the only house in town with a artificial nigger in front of it.' So I decided I would have to find a story to fit that. A little lower than starting with the theme.[9]

9. "An Interview with Flannery O'Connor and Robert Penn Warren," in *Writer to Writer*, edited by Floyd C. Watkins and Karl F. Knight (New York: Houghton Mifflin, 1966), p. 73.

Flannery at an autograph party for Wise
Blood *sponsored by the library staff of Georgia
College in 1952.*

Flannery, with Frances and Brainard ("Lon")
Cheney, 1953. She visited the Cheneys at their
home in Nashville, Tennessee. The Cheneys
were friends of Caroline Gordon, who intro-
duced them to Flannery.

As early as the 1950s Flannery O'Connor observed in her lectures and essays
that the South was getting "more like the
rest of the country" and that all too soon
there might be "no such thing as Southern literature" and very "little difference
in the end-product whether you are a
writer from Georgia or a writer from
Hollywood, California."[10] But during

10. *Mystery and Manners*, pp. 29, 57.

xxvi

O'Connor's lifetime there was a meaning-
ful difference between life in rural
Georgia and life in urban Los Angeles,
and there still is. In some sense my photographs are historical documents that give
visual permanence to the idiosyncratic es-
sence of middle Georgia before Flannery
O'Connor's prediction becomes reality.

Seeing was very important to Flannery
O'Connor. She had written that "everything has its testing point in the eye, an

Flannery, with Brainard Cheney, 1959. She was in Nashville to speak at Vanderbilt University.

Flannery, 1961, on the porch of the Cline House. The Violent Bear It Away *had been published in 1960, and she was at work on the stories later collected in* Everything That Rises Must Converge.

Flannery, 1962 or 1963. Seated on the porch of Andalusia, she poses with a portrait done by Robert Hood. She wears the same straw hat, complete with peacock feathers, that appears in the portrait.

Regina Cline O'Connor and Tom Elliot, general manager of Stone Mountain Park, 1972. Mrs. O'Connor had presented peafowl from the flock at Andalusia to the park's Game Ranch.

organ which eventually involves the whole personality and as much of the world as can be got into it." She had also insisted that the writer must "see an action, or a series of actions, clearly. The key word is *see* . . . he wants to see it himself clearly and make the reader see it clearly. . . . The fiction writer is concerned with the way the world looks first of all. He establishes it by its looks."[11]

In photographing Flannery O'Connor's Georgia I too have tried to see her world clearly, and I have tried to provide visual evidence of the world in her fiction. But the eye, of course, is my eye, and the choice of focus is mine also. "The Georgia writer's true country is not Georgia," Flannery O'Connor observed, "but Georgia is an entrance to it for him."[12] I would like my photographs to serve as document and entrance.

11. *Mystery and Manners*, p. 144; "My Mentor," p. 24.

12. From an article in the *Atlanta Constitution*, March 19, 1960.

xxx

Flannery O'Connor's Georgia

"The Georgia writer's true country is not Georgia, but Georgia is an entrance to it for him"—Flannery O'Connor.

The Georgia countryside looks much the same to me now as it did almost twenty years ago when I first visited Milledgeville. There is less space between the towns, subdivisions have divided the farms, and franchised convenience stores have replaced the country grocery. But the landscape endures: the pitted, gullied red-clay banks, the graceful formality of a pecan grove contrasting with the dark line of pine trees at the horizon, brick chimneys standing as silent

markers of vanished houses, signs nailed to trees advertising their province as Christ or a restaurant 500 yards up the road. At times the landscape plunges us into a darker agrarian past. At times the countryside oppresses. I think of John Wesley's impetuous command in "A Good Man Is Hard to Find": "Let's drive through Georgia fast so we won't have to look at it much."

These used-car bodies appeared caught in a waterless cascade made strangely beautiful by the slanting sunlight and the surrounding foliage. They belonged to the violent broken landscape perceived by Tarwater *in* The Violent Bear It Away *as he looks at the city in the indistinct light of dawn.*

"The South blossoms with every kind of complication and contradiction," Flannery O'Connor once told an Atlanta Journal-Constitution *reporter. I was intrigued by the crossing of purposes and values my camera was*

recording, and I saw in these photographs a
radical discontinuity of things that supported
O'Connor's recognition of the paradoxes of the
modern South.

Sometimes, as I traveled through middle Georgia, the patched-together stores and filling stations of the countryside outdid their fictional counterparts.

A combination grocery store and gas station comprises Goat Town. After guests had toured the Governor's Mansion and Milledgeville, Flannery O'Connor liked to take her Yankee visitors to Goat Town to show them "what the South was really like."

Stone Mountain, grey and bald, rises on the horizon a few miles outside of Atlanta. You have to climb its granite sides or view the carving of the Confederate leaders from the cable car to comprehend its monumentality. Otherwise you might as well continue reading and, like John Wesley and June Star in "A Good Man is Hard to Find," ignore its presence entirely.

Toomsboro is a small town close to Milledge-ville. With its empty stores and abandoned buildings, the town suits its name, which fore-shadows the denouement of "A Good Man is Hard to Find." I was convinced that reality is at least as strange as fiction when I saw the name of the highway that connects the two towns.

"When I went to college twenty years ago, nobody mentioned any good Southern writers to me later than Joel Chandler Harris. . . . As far as I knew, the heroes of Hawthorne and Melville and James and Crane and Hemingway were balanced on the Southern side by Brer Rabbit—an animal who can always hold up his end of the stick, in equal company, but here too much was being expected of him"
—Flannery O'Connor, "The Regional Writer."

*The Uncle Remus Museum in Eatonton is a log
cabin constructed, so the brochure says, "from
two original Putnam County slave cabins."
Flannery O'Connor described it as the only air-
conditioned slave cabin in the South.*

A view of the woods was sacred to Mary Fortune. I felt her presence as I watched this bulldozer rearrange the earth. Even the barns seemed threatened by its looming presence. Its engine throbs shattered the tranquility of the afternoon, and I regretted this intrusion in the name of progress.

A few months later, these houses were demol-
ished, the kudzu pulled up, the trees sawed
down, and a Waffle House built on the site.
Such is the fate and the glory of property ad-
joining an interstate highway.

The *J&J Brace Shop* in Macon, not far from Milledgeville, made no attempt to disguise its function or glamorize its merchandise. Its unadorned façade and window displays of wheel- chairs and prosthetic devices reminded me of the brace shop Rufus Johnson patronized so unwillingly in "The Lame Shall Enter First."

"Mine is a comic art, but that does not detract from its seriousness," Flannery O'Connor once observed, underscoring the fact that seriousness and comedy are not opposites, either in life or in fiction. Irony, which traffics in disparity, allowed her to achieve this doubleness of purpose and effect.

*Deepstep is a mile or so down the highway from
Goattown. The kaolin mining that goes on here
leaves deep exposed quarries. I find literalness
baffling and amusing. Mostly amusing.*

The white and black faces of these coachmen stared at me with equal misery and incomprehension in a grotesque and comic convergence.

The inspiration for the story "The Artificial Nigger" came from an experience of Regina O'Connor's. She stopped to ask directions and was told that her destination was easy to find: it was the only house in town to own an "artificial nigger." Flannery O'Connor was intrigued by the phrase and made up her mind to use it. "It's not only a wonderful phrase," she said, "but it's a terrible symbol of what the South has done to itself."

The farms in the fiction, like that in "The En-during Chill," are almost always versions of Andalusia with its long red clay driveway dividing the two front pastures. But life at Andalusia was more tranquil than the fictional world. Flannery O'Connor once reflected that "most of the violences carried to their logical conclusions in the stories manage to be warded off in fact here—though most of them exist in potentiality."

The farmhouse sits on the crest of the hill—a white two-story building with a wide screened porch. Andalusia to Flannery O'Connor meant solitude and rest, a place to conserve and concentrate the energy she needed for writing in the last years of her life.

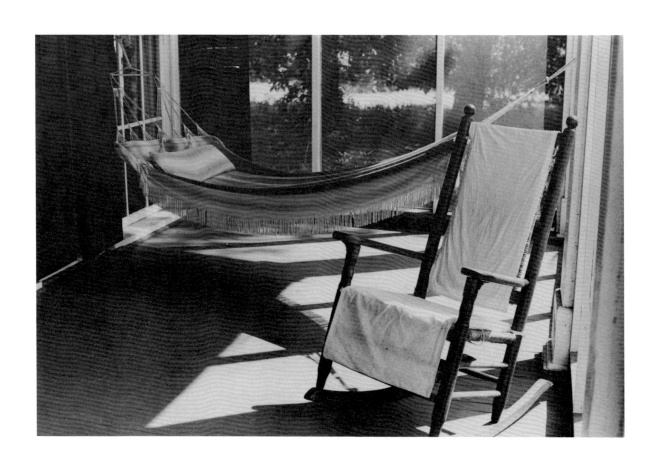

34

I met Flannery O'Connor in the "back parlor," as she liked to call it, of the farmhouse. The room was furnished with a large walnut bookcase with glass doors, a sofa placed against a far wall, occasional chairs, and tables holding books and magazines and small ornaments. The bookshelves reflected the wide range of her reading, and the ornaments and icons (some of them gifts from readers), her interest in peacocks and her Catholicism. The room was light and airy, and the space congenial to sitting and talking, or sitting and reading, or even to sitting and

watching television (a small set occupied one corner). Some of the furniture from the "back parlor" is now in the Flannery O'Connor Memorial Room at Georgia College.

The bird that shares this self-portrait is not a peacock, as many viewers assume, but a pheasant cock. Flannery O'Connor admired the fierce looks of the male pheasant with its horns and diabolical countenance. The self-portrait was done after a particularly severe siege of lupus, and the effects of cortisone and high fever are visible. "When I painted it," she said, "I didn't look either at myself in the mirror or at the bird. I knew what we both looked like."

Flannery O'Connor grew up in the Cline House, a large, antebellum house situated only a few blocks from Georgia College and downtown Milledgeville. Regina O'Connor left Andalusia and moved back to the Cline House after her daughter's death, and it was here that we met in 1968 to discuss this project. As we talked, I realized more strongly than ever the presence and influence of two Georgias in Flannery O'Connor's life. The first is the Georgia

made vivid by the fiction, the landscape I had begun to record with my camera; the second is the Georgia that she knew by birth and up-bringing, the Georgia represented by the Cline House.

41

This man admitted to being ninety. When I complimented him on his long and active life, he brought me inside his house to show me the mounted head of a deer he had shot three weeks earlier and a freezer full of venison, rabbit, and other small game.

The tractor has not rendered mules "worthless," *tisements for them are found in the* Farmer's
as Mrs. Shortley hypothesized in "The Dis- Market Bulletin, *a weekly newsletter that*
placed Person." Mules are still used to plow *Flannery O'Connor liked to read.*
and cultivate small fields, and numerous adver-

These workers were employed to pick cotton left in corners and at the end of rows and in other places inaccessible to the unwieldy mechanical pickers.

The older woman seemed as resolutely planted in the earth as the male and female scarecrows she and her daughter had put up to guard the field.

The cleanliness of her pigs was a source of pride to Mrs. Turpin in "Revelation," and she boasted that their feet never touched the ground. This pig parlor, larger than the one that housed Mrs. Turpin's pigs, was divided

into different rooms: the farrowing room, the
nursery, and the parlor proper.

Flannery O'Connor was adamant about the necessity of establishing the fictional world and its people through "its looks." She advised aspiring writers to search for whatever differentiates one person from another and to "look for this

with your eyes open, not with them shut."
My own photographs told me that Flannery
O'Connor had observed the people of her region
with her eyes wide open.

The characters in Flannery O'Connor's fiction observe each other closely and talk about each other obsessively. They seem forever amazed at the diversity of human nature and the pecu-

54

liarities of human behavior. And at those times when the multiplicity of human life becomes too complex for them, they resort to clichés and agree, as Mrs. Freeman and Mrs. Hopewell do in "Good Country People," that it takes all kinds to make the world.

The Southern black male, Flannery O'Connor told C. Ross Mullins in an interview for **Jubilee,** *is "a man of very elaborate manners and great formality, which he uses superbly for his own protection and to insure his own privacy. . . . It requires considerable grace for two races to live together, particularly when the population is divided about 50–50 between*

them and when they have our particular history. It can't be done without a code of manners based on mutual charity. . . . The South has survived in the past because its manners, however lopsided or inadequate they may have been, provided enough social discipline to hold us together and give us an identity."

*Jesus assumes a literal presence in the South,
and I like to think of him as Haze Motes in
Wise Blood did: a wild and ragged figure
moving from tree to tree in the back of his
mind, always there, always beckoning, always*

shaping his thoughts and destiny. "While the South is hardly Christ-centered," Flannery O'Connor said, "it is most certainly Christ-haunted."

The insistent signs nailed on pine trees or posts asked as well as answered questions about life and eternity, and I thought of Rufus Johnson in "The Lame Shall Enter First," who was destined to "know the Bible with or without reading it."

 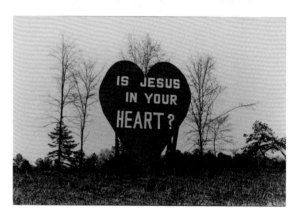

Entertainer, man of God, salesman, this preacher held his power in his tongue, his neck, and arm.

Unlike Haze Motes, who from childhood knew that he was destined to be a preacher, this man did not receive his calling until his early thirties. By day he worked in a chemical plant; at night and on the weekend he preached the word of God. Here, at the end of a service, he lays hands on a worshipper open and eager to receive the spirit of the Lord.

70

tism led the young boy carefully into the river, measuring its depth with the stick he carried.

Before immersing the child, he covered the boy's eyes with a cloth handkerchief. I liked the

proud look of the newly baptized boy as he stood
with his family.

I had never attended a Pentecostal service until I began to photograph for this book. I knew that Flannery O'Connor viewed her "backwoods prophets" and other religious enthusiasts seriously and saw their concerns as paralleling her own and being "central to human life." I wanted to experience this realization for myself. My conversations with the Holiness people,

the sermons and testimonies I heard, and those moments when a spiritual presence was felt in the tent gave me insight into and respect for a religious expression alien to my subdued Presbyterian childhood. I then began to understand the fiction more deeply.

I took this photograph at a tent meeting led by a black evangelist and his wife. When this white woman came forth to testify, I thought of "Everything That Rises Must Converge" and of Pierre Teilhard de Chardin's postulation of a final convergence in Christ of all life at the omega point and silently applauded this spiritual convergence on earth.

Of all the farm and barnyard animals, Flannery O'Connor liked the peafowl the most, and the flock at Andalusia grew to more than forty. They seemed to be everywhere, resting on fenceposts and rooftops, in the driveways, on the lawns, even adorning the front steps. They were noisy, messy, domineering, and majestic, creatures at once foolish and magnificent, inhabitors of the barnyard and the bird of Hera, canny and uncanny.

"I intend to stand firm and let the peacocks multiply, for I am sure that, in the end, the last word will be theirs" —Flannery O'Connor, "The King of Birds."